Pets at My House

Cats

Jennifer Blizin Gillis

Heinemann Library
Chicago, Illinois

Page layout by Kim Kovalick, Heinemann Library
Printed and bound in China by South China Printing Company Limited.
Photo research by Jill Birschbach

08
10 9 8 7 6 5 4 3
Library of Congress Cataloging-in-Publication Data

Gillis, Jennifer Blizin, 1950-
    Cats / Jennifer Blizin Gillis.
        p. cm. -- (Pets at my house)
    Includes index.
    ISBN 1-4034-5051-X (hc) -- ISBN 1-4034-6019-1 (pbk.)
    ISBN 978-1-4034-5051-7 (hc) -- ISBN 978-1-4034-6019-6 (pbk.)
    1. Cats--Miscellanea--Juvenile literature. I. Title. II. Series.
    SF445.7.G56 2004
    636.8--dc22   2004002469

Acknowledgments

The author and publishers are grateful to the following for permission to reproduce copyright material:

Cover photograph by Scott Braut

pp. 4, 14, 15, 16, 17, back cover Greg Williams/Heinemann Library; p. 5 Jill Birschbach/Heinemann Library; pp. 6, 8 Dwight Kuhn; p. 7l Digital Vision/Getty Images; pp. 7r, 10, 11, 12, 13, 20, 21 Scott Braut; p. 9 Tudor Photography/Heinemann Library; p. 18 Renee Stockdale/Animals Animals; pp. 19, 22 Dave Bradford/Heinemann Library; p. 23 (from T-B) Dave Bradford/Heinemann Library, Greg Williams/Heinemann Library, Greg Williams/Heinemann Library, Dwight Kuhn, Greg Williams/Heinemann Library

Every effort has been made to contact copyright holders of any material reproduced in this book. Any omissions will be rectified in subsequent printings if notice is given to the publisher.

Special thanks to our advisory panel for their help in the preparation of this book:

Alice Bethke,
Library Consultant
Palo Alto, CA

Kathleen Gilbert,
Second Grade Teacher
Round Rock, TX

Jan Gobeille, Kindergarten Teacher
Garfield Elementary
Oakland, CA

Eileen Day,
Preschool Teacher
Chicago, IL

Sandra Gilbert,
Library Media Specialist
Fiest Elementary School
Houston, TX

Angela Leeper,
Educational Consultant
Wake Forest, NC

Contents

Some words are shown in bold, **like this.**
You can find them in the picture glossary on page 23.

What Kind of Pet Is This?

Pets are animals that live with us.

Some pets are small and slippery.

My pet is small and hairy.

Can you guess what kind of
pet it is?

What Are Cats?

Cats are **mammals.**

Mammals make milk for their babies.

There are big cats in the wild.

But most cats are small and live with people.

Where Did My Cat Come From?

A mother cat had a litter of kittens.

At first, the kittens could not see.

They stayed with their mother for eight weeks.

Then, I took one of the kittens home.

How Big Is My Cat?

At first, my kitten was as small as your hand.

It weighed as much as a small bag of sugar.

Now my kitten is a cat.

It is about as big as a pair of shoes.

Where Does My Cat Live?

My cat lives in the house with us.

It does not need a special house.

My cat has a bed.

It is soft and round.

What Does My Cat Eat?

My cat eats dry cat food.

Sometimes it eats fish, too.

I always give it water to drink.

Sometimes I give my cat treats.

What Else Does My Cat Need?

My cat needs a **litter box.**

It is like a cat toilet.

My cat needs a **collar** and nametag.

These can help me find my cat if it gets lost.

What Can I Do for My Cat?

I play with my cat everyday.

Playing is good exercise for cats.

I brush my cat everyday.

Brushing keeps my cat's **coat** shiny.

What Can My Cat Do?

My cat is strong.

It can jump high.

My cat is smart.

It knows how to open doors.

Cat Map

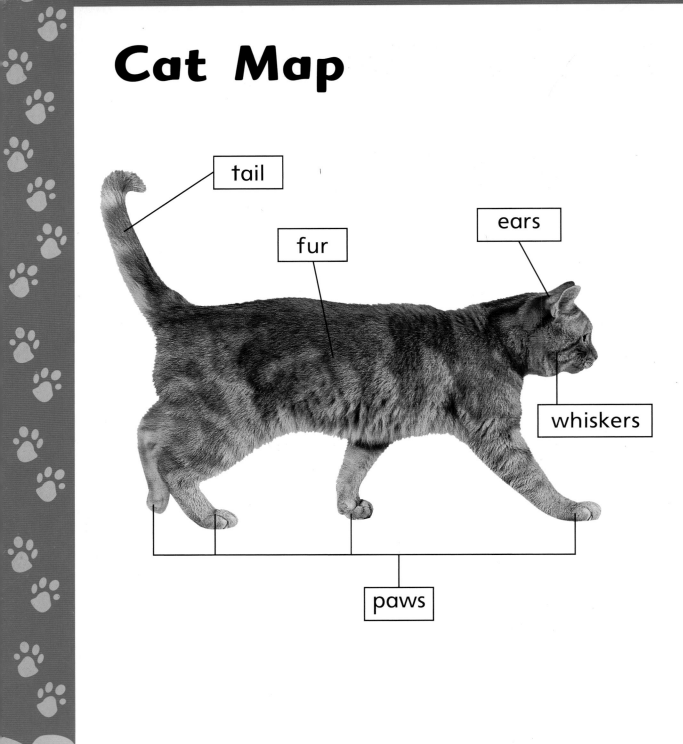

tail

fur

ears

whiskers

paws

Picture Glossary

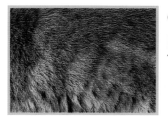

coat
page 19
thick hair or fur that covers an animal's body

collar
page 17
cloth or leather band a pet wears around its neck

litter box
page 16
small box cats use as a toilet

mammal
page 6
animal that has hair or fur and that makes milk for its babies

Note to Parents and Teachers

Reading for information is an important part of a child's literacy development. Learning begins with a question about something. Help children think of themselves as investigators and researchers by encouraging their questions about the world around them. Each chapter in this book begins with a question. Read the question together. Look at the pictures. Talk about what you think the answer might be. Then read the text to find out if your predictions were correct. Think of other questions you could ask about the topic, and discuss where you might find the answers. Assist children in using the picture glossary and the index to practice new vocabulary and research skills.

! CAUTION: Remind children to be careful when handling animals. Pets may scratch or bite if startled. Children should wash their hands with soap and water after they touch any animal.

Index